CASSOULET
a french obsession

by **KATE HILL** & photographs by **TIM CLINCH**

TO MOM

Text copyright © 2015 Kate Hill

Photographs copyright © Tim Clinch Photography

Text editing by Nathan Gilmour, Katie Hunter, and Anita Crotty

Book design by Meghan Hildebrand

ISBN 978-0-692-77339-0

Printed in China

Published by Rancho Gordo New World Specialty Food
1924 Yajome Street
Napa, CA 94559

www.ranchogordo.com

CONTENTS

What I remember most about the first night I ever tried Kate's cassoulet—or any cassoulet, for that matter—was the light. We had set a huge wooden door on sawhorses in the stone barn next to her house, surrounded by every chair, stool, or box we could find. Dominique and the family were coming over, the students, the neighbors, and of course Kate's dog, Bacon. It was cold in the cavernous elemental space, the only thing cutting the crisp in the air was the heap of candles twisting their light across the wooden surface. Backlit by the flames, the carafes of wine took on a ruby glow, the faces of the guests ochre ovals bowing in from the darkness. The night grew longer and the *aperitifs* dwindled as we waited for the main event: the burbling, crispy cassoulet. The deep, meaty fragrance hit you first, with wave after wave of sensory joy following closely behind to bowl you right over. The faces were closer now, eyes, noses, and tongues divining the space, embers in the darkness, our backs straining against the cold. Then the steam erupted from the jagged crater as Kate finally broke the surface of her magic cassoulet and all was right that night in the barn at Camont.

— Nathan Gilmour
Camont, November 2015

I met Kate Hill many years ago in New Orleans. I knew immediately that she was a woman following her passions and her real joy was sharing these passions with other people. We were at Donald Link's celebrated Cochon restaurant and she dug into each dish with so much infectious enthusiasm that by the end of the meal we were all nearly experts in the art of charcuterie.

She approaches the classic cassoulet with the same love and dedication, and again, her enthusiasm is infectious. I would find it hard to believe that you won't feel you're somewhat of a cassoulet expert by the time you reach the end of this book. You will be calling good friends to come join you at the table to celebrate your victory in the kitchen. And I hope, as you're raising a toast, you'll take a moment to remember Kate. For me, she's a key ingredient in any classic cassoulet.

— Steve Sando

Kate Hill has lived in Southwest France—the birthplace of cassoulet—for several decades. In this book, she shares her extensive knowledge of the subject, just as if she were sitting at the table with you, sharing a meal and telling stories.

When Kate came to my house in California to make cassoulet with me, Steve Sando, and a small group of friends, I asked her what I needed to gather ahead of time, expecting an extensive list of esoteric ingredients. Instead she said, "Oh, some beans—Tarbais if you can get them—carrots, celery, leeks, onions, parsley, thyme, bay leaves. You know, the usual vegetables and herbs. Some duck leg confit, a few sausages, and if you can get some pork belly that would be great. Otherwise, don't worry about it." Well, I thought to myself, this sounds pretty doable. And it was.

Steve brought a couple of pounds of his Rancho Gordo Cassoulet beans, and I supplied the rest. We chopped and simmered and chatted. We eventually chose a slope-sided Le Creuset Dutch oven for the baking, and seared the meats in a skillet on top of the stove. Beans and meats were then layered in the pot and baked until a golden crust formed on the top.

By lunchtime, the cassoulet was ready to serve. We ate it under the big black walnut tree in my backyard, along with baguettes and wine and a gratin made with chard from my garden. It was a classic French Sunday lunch. Honest food, simply made, with lots of good conversation. Of course, Kate, an expert on all things cassoulet, regaled us with stories of more elaborate versions and multiple variations of the famous dish, but we happily enjoyed what was before us.

— Georgeanne Brennan, author of
A Pig in Provence and *La Vie Rustic*

A heavy bowl, full to the brim with steaming beans and cured meats, blanketed by a golden filigree of crust, resting on my kitchen table. This image, my friends, is my inspiration for this book.

Cassoulet is the culinary equivalent of turning straw into gold. Though its alchemy is complex, the process is not complicated. A clear idea of what you are trying to create, and the means to get there, is all you need to satisfy your craving.

I have tried to steer clear of murky historical references and, instead, share with you my personal way of making delicious cassoulet. In order to demystify the culinary alchemist's secrets, I share with you the basic and simple ingredients needed to produce one of France's most beloved national treasures: cassoulet.

— Kate Hill

STORIES

A FRENCH OBSESSION WITH BEANS, BONES & BROTH

The history of cassoulet is rich in written sources that are quoted, requoted, and misquoted. Cassoulet has had its origins attributed variously to seventh-century Arabs, the Hundred Years War (early 1300s), and the bourgeois home cooking of nineteenth-century France. Some say cassoulet is influenced by either North Africa's lamb and beans, or neighboring Catalunya's fava bean stews. Modernists claim New World beans gave birth to cassoulet in the 1700s; food historians know that fava beans and other Old World legumes like *pois carré* (cow peas) were cooked as a staple diet throughout the Mediterranean basin from antiquity. There are abundant and conflicting written references and theories about every aspect of this favored dish, from the etymology of the word cassoulet to the dish in which it is cooked, called a *cassole*.

However, by the early twentieth century, cassoulet had been written down in the official codes of French gastronomy, frozen in time. France's current obsession with cassoulet—well-documented on television, websites, and blogs—reflects the contemporary luxury of time, as we call family and friends to the table to rediscover the roots of good food. We respond to the abundant and convivial winter table where we gather together to talk, as much as practice, a sanctioned national pastime: gastronomy.

France's national obsession with food both reflects and empowers the diversity of her many regions. Local food festivals are held across the country celebrating everything from walnuts to tomatoes, from cheese to—of course—cassoulet. North to south, Napoleon might have unified France under one flag and one language, but French regions remain fiercely allegiant to their local dishes. All of France might recognize cassoulet as a quintessentially French dish, but it is in the Languedoc—the southeast of the Southwest, where a renewed interest in the Occitan language and music thrives—that cassoulet militants stand behind a particular bean or certain shaped pot.

I recently sat at a cafe in Castelnaudary listening to a debate about the merits of the lozenge-shaped Lingot bean versus the fat, kidney-shaped Tarbais bean. Over a glass of Minervois wine, I wondered why cassoulet inspired such impassioned discourse. After all, it's just beans and meat. Then I looked outside the cafe windows, saw the howling Tramontane wind sweeping leather-like, hand-size leaves across the square and remembered my own first memorable encounters with cassoulet, decades ago.

MY OBSESSION BEGINS

Cassoulet season usually arrives with the first frosty mornings of early November as the plane trees along the Canal du Midi in Southwest France carpet the still water's surface with large golden leaves. The clay-rich fields of the great Lauragais Plain are now bare after their year's work of growing seeds: wheat, sunflowers, corn, chicory. The insistent wind, called Tramontane, is gathering force for its brusque challenges; the air is clear and chilled. The southern French sun is still strong but winter foods that warm the core are welcome now. A Sunday morning stroll across a bare cornfield provides a hare or a pheasant; the long-simmering hours of food on a hearth provide the family table with comfort. The winter passes and yet it was in the spring that I learned to make cassoulet here in Southwest France like I learned the language—through culinary immersion.

I arrived in Castelnaudary on my canal barge, the *Julia Hoyt,* one cold March day during a rare snowstorm. It was 1988 and I was 37 years old. My French adventure had just begun. Taking respite from the strong Midi winds, my mates and I sailed across the choppy Grand Bassin at Castelnaudary, ricocheted through a very small bridge and into the calmer waters of the back port. We thought to moor for a few days, weeks, whatever. This was life on a barge. We moved when we pleased. We stayed some months.

Sailing across France from top to bottom I had already eaten *pain d'epice* in Dijon, *boudin blanc* in Rethel, and *coq au vin* in Burgundy. But I had never encountered such a food obsession as cassoulet. Fueled by rival cloaked and hooded "gangs" called *confreries* or The Academy, cassoulet seemed to create a fervor for regional food that is only equaled by local rugby supporters.

I visited Toulouse's charming brick city center and walked the ramparts of Carcassonne, inhaling the medieval ambiance in every souvenir shop, but I found Castelnaudary's claim to fame to be singular—cassoulet. Just cassoulet. *Le vrai cassoulet.* Shop signs, butcher shops, charcuteries, *traiteurs,* and *cassouletiers* sport the same iconic emblem: a flared, open terracotta pot with a double lip and small pouring spout—a *cassole.* Like in a game of I Spy, I counted more than a dozen *cassoles* hand painted on signs, glazed into tiles, and hanging in ironwork on the main street alone. This was truly the home of cassoulet.

Some believe that Toulouse and Carcassonne perpetually compete for the 'best' cassoulet in the Southwest, but Castelnaudary is so dedicated to the dish that the town painted its water tower to resemble a giant *cassole*. So today, in this book, I leave the other historical references behind and begin with a very personal look at modern cassoulet.

Like most other regional French cooking, cassoulet has been associated with a specific point of geography. (See the next chapter, Terroir of Southwest France.) Coco beans are grown in Pamiers; Tarbais beans come from Tarbes; Lingots grow throughout the Lauragais Plain. So as each small tribe of good cooks claimed a point of difference—a certain bean, a type of meat, the shape of the *cassole*—the cassoulet wars began. Bean-and-meat dishes are legion. But what was it that inspired rival recipes to compete for the best, the most authentic, the real cassoulet, as if there could only be **one** cassoulet in a country of 65 million food critics?

Actually, it wasn't obvious how to learn to make cassoulet while living in Castelnaudary, since half of the town does it for a living. Why go through all the bother at home when beautiful small shops, busy wood-oven cafes, white-tablecloth restaurants, and even huge industrial factories are dedicated to perfecting the recipe? One can stop and order any size cassoulet—a 10-person, 6-person, or even a very generous 2-person version—already cooked, complete with perfect crusty top, ready to go.

In those early days, every time I traveled through Castelnaudary on the Canal du Midi, I'd cradle a heavy full *cassole* on the back of my bike, returning to the galley of the *Julia Hoyt* to reheat it until it was bubbled and brown on the top. I'd proudly serve it to my guests with a big green salad and pour a bottle of strong red wine from the Minervois. *Eh voilà*, true French cassoulet! I didn't begin making my own cassoulet until I found my own kitchen a few years later and left my barging days behind.

Since France has codified Cassoulet with a capital C, you think they'd all turn out the same: dried beans, some form of pork and other meat, and the usual flavor trio of bay, garlic, and onion cooked for hours in an oven. However, after eating cassoulet across the whole of the Lauragais Plain—good, bad, and indifferent—I was challenged to decipher an elemental cassoulet. One of the best and one of the worst cassoulets were eaten in the same acclaimed restaurant in the same year. How far we fall from the sublime to the undercooked!

I became obsessed with understanding the "why behind the how" of cassoulet; I decided to take matters in my own hand and create the best cassoulet in my own kitchen. I started Camp Cassoulet at Camont, a way to banish the winter blues, warm the hearth, and call in far-flung friends to celebrate a new season: The Cassoulet Season. It was a good excuse as any to test recipes and make multiple cassoulets all at once. We swapped beans and changed the meat, cooked on an open hearth, in the electric stove, and in a small wood-burning oven. I began to use cassoulet as a verb, cassoulet-ing dozens of different recipes and countless kilos of beans of many varieties.

Cassoulet as the object of my own obsession took a boost from the abundance of great charcuterie I was producing with my butchery students here at Camont. Cassoulet is the perfect all-in-one dish to showcase both beans and good charcuterie, from ham to *confit de canard*. Those umami-rich flavors of good pork and duck charcuterie comingle with the simple nourishing bean (in both a supportive and starring role) to create a third, separate flavor experience. This alchemy satisfies the spirit and elevates a simple plate to a world-class dish. In other words, cassoulet.

For centuries, French housewives made cassoulet with what they had at hand and without a written recipe. I can't imagine anyone intended for there to be hard, fast rules that limited your own cooking experience. But they did have three advantages over you: eyes in France, a nose in France and—best of all—a mouth in France. So let me be your cassoulet guide, here in Southwest France, and share this simple French obsession with you.

TERROIR OF SOUTHWEST FRANCE

Terroir—sense of place, love of the land—is everything in France. It is the tangible and natural anchor for this well-defined nation and the people who defend its borders from the global invasion of pop culture. From outside France, its Southwest is a vague, sunny, rural landscape peopled by heroic mustachioed swash-bucklers and a jovial monarchy stuck somewhere firmly in the Middle Ages. From within France, it's not much different. Parisians see Southwest France as a sunflower-strewn vacationland, a land of abundant milk, honey, and Armagnac. It is the ideal birthplace where all iconic *grand-meres* learn to cook and people take the time to sit at long tables for hours and hours. Within our own secluded personal corner, terroir defines the wines we drink, the food we eat, and the way we live. Somehow it all works together.

Southwest France stretches between two seas, from the Atlantic Ocean to the Mediterranean. It is capped by snow-peaked Pyrenees to the south and hemmed in to the north by the Massif Centrale plateau. With a diverse and rich agricultural history supported by royal decree as early as the fifteenth century, Southwest France still holds food traditions and culinary lore firmly at the heart of its modern culture. Today we celebrate a dish whose origins are lost in antiquity, muddled by wars, and defined by em-battled factions. And yet it continues to hold sway over the entire country as emblematic of the best of French cooking: Cassoulet, a daughter of Southwestern terroir.

Terroir is an amalgamation of many things that affect the good foodstuffs grown in Southwest France: sunlight, rainfall, daylight hours, soil quality, and the gentle lay of the land as it stretches between two maritime influences. Here, I also include the human touch under terroir: The long agricultural traditions and culture that support growth, quality, and the value of excellent materials; the husbandry and midwifery that have tended this land for so many centuries. Terroir should also include an elusive and intangi-ble element: Time, measured in slow-growing seasons so that ani-mals, as well as vegetables, benefit from a full, fat life to develop deep flavor and nutritional qualities.

Factory-farmed pig, pushed to adolescent slaughter to render pale pink pork, doesn't belong in the charcuterie I make for this cassoulet. A strong-boned farm duck fatted on local grain is the result of the terroir that encourages the growing of cereals in broad strokes of these fertile river valleys. In France, terroir is evident in every kitchen and implicit in every recognized regional dish from Burgundy's *coq au vin* and Alsace's *choucroute garni* to Southwest France's cassoulet, *garbure* and *poule-au-pot*.

I believe in terroir with all the fervor and passion of a religious convert. I claim my adopted corner of the French hexagram with a level of enthusiasm usually reserved for winning sports teams—GO FAT DUCKS!—or political rallies—YES, WE CA...SSOULET! I am sublimely aware—every hour of the day, every day of the rolling seasons—that I live in one of most delicious, diverse, and fruitful places on the earth: Southwest France. And I remember to say *"merci!"* to the gods of happenstance. That summer the barge's transmission broke down and we tugged the *Julia Hoyt* along the towpath into Agen, I had my first encounters with terroir as I shopped for my floating kitchen.

In France, and especially in Southwest France, there is a palpable pride attributed to terroir. A pride that comes from knowing intimately the land and the patterns of sun and wind, or summer rain and spring frosts, that make their mark on all things grown within its reach. When I drink a rare wine from 1989, I remember how wonderfully hot it was that summer, how we swam in the canal to cool ourselves down while the Buzet grapes worked overtime to become a starred vintage. When I make a slice of toast for breakfast on a late and rainy spring day, I know that the farmers who planted the wheat watch the same rain that waters my own little *potager* garden. I like knowing this land so intimately but I love knowing the people that turn this rich alluvial valley into food. This is terroir taken to the highest degree.

CASSOLE. CAÇOLA. CASSEROLE.

Does the dish make the dish?

Cassoulet is named after its baking dish: in French, *cassole*, and in Occitan, *cuçola*. Just like other important national dishes from tagines to terrines, form doesn't just follow function. It often dictates content and how we perceive the finished dish.

The origins of the recipe are as contested as the etymology of the word for the pot itself: *cassole*. Let us agree to agree that the name for *cassole* is buried in old Spanish and Occitan words used for a cooking vessel and reflect a common history with other similar words for dishes like *caçola, cassa, cazuela* and casserole. From *cassole* was born cassoulet.

If the pot comes first in naming the dish, then it stands to reason it is as important as the ingredients themselves. What makes cassoulet such an iconic French dish, so easily recognized from a table away, is the pot as much as what goes in to it. Its distinctive shape is hand-thrown of thick refractory clay to form a basin deep enough to keep the contents moist yet with a large enough opening to encourage a slow-baked crust. It is clear that cassoulet was always baked in an oven rather than cooked over a stove or in an open fire. The dish itself defines that. A *cassole* begs for an oven and the cassoulet it delivers is the proof.

Traditional *cassoles* have a narrow base, deep enough to hold a large volume of beans, meat, and broth. The heavy clay bowl flares out to a wide rim; two sturdy handles are attached to help make it easier to retrieve the hot *cassole* from the oven. The final personal touch is the potter's thumbprint: a pouring spout.

As ripe for controversy as any one element of cassoulet, the *cassole* itself is its own jousting point between differing factions. But let me stop you before you begin to question whether you can even begin tackling cassoulet if you don't have the anointed pot. I have made cassoulet in aluminum restaurant pans and cast-iron Dutch ovens; in stainless steel, enamel, and tinfoil pans. In electric and gas ovens, over open coals, and in wood-burning bread ovens. They were all different and all delicious.

But the best cassoulet I make is in my large Poterie Not Frères *cassole* that I have seasoned with cassoulet lore and love for more than 30 years. It serves 10 to 12 people and stays hot until the second helpings go around. It stands at the heart of the table and spouts steam like an upside-down volcano.

Remember, just like any of the other essential ingredients, choosing your baking vessel carefully is the key. Understand the reason why we choose a particular element and you can duplicate, vary, create, or riff on your own *cassole* later.

To be a true *cassole*, the vessel must:

- Be deep
- Be wider than it is tall
- Be thick- and even-walled
- Be made of heat-loving material, such as clay
- Have a small pouring spout
- Have two sturdy, simple handles.

PORTRAIT OF THE POTERIE NOT FRÈRES

I encountered my first *cassole* as I sailed the Canal du Midi in 1988. Upon discovering the several cassoulet takeout shops in Castelnaudary, I bought a cassoulet, big enough to feed 10 people, from the Art Nouveau wooden-facaded Maison Escudier. I balanced it on my bicycle back to my barge, moored in the town's spacious port. I was delighted to take the precooked cassoulet back to the galley to feed my friends and shipmates. Equally delighting me was, that for a very small sum, I now owned this beautiful big pot! I don't really remember the small fee I paid as a deposit on the deep brown glazed bowl, but it was inconsequential enough that I decided that I would keep the *cassole* and forfeit the deposit. Who knew when I would encounter another lovely big bowl like this?

Actually, the next encounter was the very next day. As I left the Grand Bassin along Pierre-Paul Riquet's curvaceous Canal du Midi, and was beginning to have cassoulet withdrawals, I ran smack into the secret heart of the recipe perched on the towpath by l'Ecluse de la Mediterranean, the canal lock next to the Poterie Not Frères. We slowly approached the vine-covered bridge and poked our long nose under it. Then I spotted the towering chimney and small squat workshop of the Not brothers. I jumped ship at the lock and ran over to investigate as the barge rose up the last level of canal to the waiting summit.

Oh. My. God. The Pots! Hundreds of pots. Small, medium, and large. Wet, dry, and fired. Brown, green, and yellow. So this is where my *cassole* had been made! There were two brothers and a young boy working side by side in silence, with the exception of whirring pottery wheels and a small clay-encrusted radio whistling the French news from an equally slip-covered shelf. Two dusty workers out back mixed water and dirt, making clay and extruding it on ancient machinery.

The Poterie Not Frères still perches along the canal like a fire-belching guardian; the tall brick chimney from the old wood-fired kiln watches over the small bridge leading to the last lock on the upstream side of the canal. Continually active since 1850s, the pottery was acquired by Emile Not in the 1940s and has produced hand-thrown *cassoles* ever since.

I met the second generation Not brothers, Aimé and Robert, on that virgin cassoulet cruise from Castelnaudary in the late 1980s. I fell in love with the quiet whirring of potter's wheels, the pink powdery clay-covered doors and windows, the shadowed light that made each potter into a Caravaggio portrait. Then I fell for the gentle men that would talk, turn, and work as they welcomed a steady stream of visitors into their workshop.

There is no shop to speak of; they work mostly for orders from restaurants and shops, but they will stop their pot-throwing production long enough to add up a few cherished purchases chosen from the overstock room. To my great delight the last time I visited, and just prior to taking these photographs, I found a small treasure of dark-green and yellow-ochre soup plates. I filled the back of the car and returned to Camont, knowing they were perfect for serving cassoulet at the table.

As much as the recipe itself, the terracotta pots made at Poterie Not Frères reflect the terroir of cassoulet. Pulled from the earth at their own quarry at nearby Issel, the clay is cleaned and transformed out back, the cassoles are then thrown, dried, glazed, fired, and sold on site. In the heart of Cassoulet country at Mas Ste.-Puelles, the Not family—father, brothers, and now cousins Jean-Pierre and Phillipe—

have been keeping the business of making cassoles alive, from earth to table.

Since that first long-ago day, I have bought more than my fair share of hand-thrown pots, cruchots (or water jugs), umbrella stands, and garden urns from Aimé, his brother Robert, and now their sons. I have photographed, filmed, talked, and coerced with a bottle of Armagnac until I learned a few secrets, had a bigger picture, and could count them as friends.

But most important of all, that day, I learned to value how a simple vessel would inspire my cassoulet endeavors for a couple decades: a thick-walled, hand-thrown clay pot with sturdy lip and pouring spout could sit in an oven for hours and hours, all the while cradling the beans as they plump in their own delicious juices.

INGREDIENTS

THE BASICS

There is nothing so special or expensive in these ingredients to scare you away. I have cooked and taught classes on several different continents and, with a little creative shopping or bartering, have found all I needed to create an authentic version of France's delicious national obsession, cassoulet.

A cassoulet is made of three essential ingredients: beans, bones/meat, and broth. At first in a pot on the stove, then later in a slow oven, these key players meld into a new entity whose distinct parts are now changed into a single, whole universe. At heart, cassoulet, like terroir itself, is an amalgamation of just a few essential and base ingredients: dried beans, salted meat, and water. When combined under the attention of a careful cook, these culinary elements fuse into a dish whose influence on our palate and spirit is greater than the sum of its individual parts.

Technique counts as far as cooking times and seasoning and there are lots of *trucs*—that delightful French word for clever tricks or inspired shortcuts—that I share in the recipes. However, without carefully chosen ingredients, technique is just an empty exercise. Each simple ingredient plays a key role, a critical part, that allows it to transform the others within the earthenware pot into a transcendental dish.

It all begins with each individual ingredient. Before we can talk substitutions and variations, we must understand the role that each product plays. We must know the essence of each element before we can swap it out for something different.

Cassoulet is perfect pantry food. Stock your own larder, even if it is just one shelf in your apartment kitchen. Buy good fresh beans from a reliable source (see Beans, page 49) and store them carefully. Put up some meat preserved exclusively for this purpose: *confit de canard,* dried ham hocks, a few tails and trotters you've frozen from other meals. Gather fresh herbs and dry them yourself; when you want thyme, lovage, and bay leaf, they are reasonably vigorous. Always have good cooking carrots, pungent onions, and fresh garlic at hand. Cooking from the pantry might be Old World thinking, but ultimately it makes modern cooking easier.

From the bean to the pot, the final cassoulet is only as good as its respective parts. Simply put, to make a great cassoulet one must begin with great ingredients.

BEANS

It's really all about the beans.

We all know that cassoulet is primarily a bean dish. Without the beans, there's no cassoulet. Beans are the true *raison d'etre* for cassoulet. Beans provide flavor, body, and nutrients. After all, cassoulet is food, not just a culinary showpiece.

Essentially a peasant dish, cassoulet is based on the sort of wintry, hearty, calorie-dense food that feeds large families, small armies, and public gatherings. Beans make that possible. Beans offer high food value for a low cost, and are an easy way to spread the more meager meat-wealth around.

Today's versions of gourmet cassoulet are often so meat-heavy that the bean becomes just a bit player, the chorus for all the rich charcuterie stars. My exemplary cassoulet keeps the bean at the base of the pyramid, so I choose my building blocks with care.

RULE #1: BUY GOOD BEANS.

It's that simple. Good beans are probably more difficult to find than all the meaty parts you can source in any decent deli. It's worth a little extra effort to find good beans and using the following criteria, you can make better decisions.

So, what's a good bean?

Fresh beans are essential.

Flavor is critical.

Local is nice, whenever possible.

Size and variety count.

FRESH. How can a dried bean be fresh? Steve Sando, the legume lover behind Rancho Gordo Heirloom Beans, considers dried beans fresh for up to 2 years. Imagine if you took that little bean and planted it in a nice warm garden and watered it. Is it still viable? Will it still grow a plant? Is the germ (its life force) still active in its dormant stage? That's a fresh bean!

After 2 years—and especially when stored badly—beans start to die, become difficult to cook, taste like starch, and lose some of their nutritional value.

Check the sell-by date. Look for the harvest year. Or, better yet, grow some in your garden plot. Fresh beans, just picked from the vine, have the same sweet quality as corn or potatoes. A good bean supplier will assure you of freshness.

FLAVOR. You might be surprised to hear that beans have flavor. Yes, beans are the main flavor in cassoulet! If you don't pay attention here, you are sunk. Beans are more flavorful when fresh but they also vary in flavor like they do in color, size, shape, skin thickness, and texture. Imagine a plump, creamy-centered Borlotti and small black Cuban bean. They taste as different as they look.

When I began documenting these cassoulet chronicles, I bought a variety of locally available French beans and ordered beans from Ranch Gordo online. Then I did a flavor-and-texture test by cooking a cup of each variety, by itself, in plain boiling water. I found my favorite, the "beaniest" ones, and made those my go-to selections. Develop your bean tastebuds by experimenting.

LOCAL. Beans that haven't traveled far have a lot working for them. Here in Southwest France, there are several variety of white beans grown that are favored for cassoulet: Lingot, Tarbais, Coco. These regional beans rely on the soil and climate to create a distinct taste of terroir. It is said that hot and dry summers, like those of Southwest France, affect the quality of the beans; a short growing cycle produces a stable and creamy bean.

Both the Tarbais and the Coco de Pamiers nearly became extinct in Southwest France by the end of the last century. Saved by local agriculture cooperatives, these beans have boosted the local agriculture as well as adding to cassoulet's regional cachet.

I favor a "love the one you're with" attitude about beans. Cassoulet made in Castelnaudary often uses Lingots that grow nearby; a Toulouse restaurant might rely on Tarbais; and housewives across Gascony find Coco de Pamiers at the local supermarket. I buy fresh Coco beans in September in 10 kg sacks, shell them myself, then can or freeze them. Fresh beans, not fully dried, seem more tender and complex than dried beans. Years where I have good garden karma, I grow beans of many varieties and make summer cassoulet straight from the vines. Buying local, like with any food product, usually means a fresher, more economical, and community-supportive decision. It also means I know my source and my product better.

Shopping for beans is like walking through a minefield of global pitfalls and issues. When I was cooking cassoulet in New Zealand, where they don't seem to grow any beans, I found all imported dried beans were irradiated. They seemed tough and harder to cook. Was that because of the irradiation process? The age of the beans? Or a simple storage issue? I read labels and made phone calls and finally settled for organic white kidney beans grown in China.

Here in France at the supermarkets, I find dried beans from China or Argentina, too. If I want locally grown—and I do!—I have to search through the village markets for a producer. The national supermarkets don't stock local beans. However, I am lucky there are several small producers who have jumped on the bean wagon and are within shopping distance each week.

Ordering beans online from a reliable source is another good option. Look for provenance and date of harvest as the world of variety opens up. I know and trust Rancho Gordo's heirloom beans because I know its owner, Steve Sando. It's like knowing my local producers at the Nerac market, only farther away. When I travel in the U.S., I usually get Steve to ship beans ahead wherever I am cooking and eliminate the bad bean blues.

SIZE AND VARIETY. This is as much about texture as taste; it is an important element in the overall experience of cassoulet. I like my cassoulet to brag about its distinct parts, with the star bean dictating the supporting characters' roles and the number of people I am serving.

> **Large:** My first choice for a big cassoulet is the Tarbais. I love the pearly white beans, as big as my thumb, and they sit well on a plate with a large *saucisse de Toulouse* and chunk of duck confit. Grown on poles and netting on small farms in the Bearn, they need to be hand harvested and their price reflects this. At some supermarkets in France, I find them for €9 for 500 g, about twice the price of the same variety grown locally and sold by Madame Borde at the Nerac market. I support all the local bean collectives; without them, these lovely white buttons of goodness would have disappeared completely within my own lifetime. And I grow them, too, along with other colorful bean varieties in my own *potager* at Camont. They seem to accept the rich clay soil and thrive under long summer days. I let them dry on the vine under the late August sun before harvesting.

> **Medium:** Next, I prefer the fat, creamy pillows called Coco de Pamiers for a summer cassoulet. These beans, too, were nearly extinct by the mid-1980s. Now they are thriving in the rich river valley of the Ariege, south of Castelnaudary, husbanded by a group of ardent bean growers. Low-growing bush beans, Coco are harvested in mid-to-late summer while still fresh in the pod; they are also available dried for winter use and they make a grand cassoulet. In this same category, Great Northern, White Kidney, and Cannellini beans all work well for cassoulet. However, given the great heirloom varieties of brown or speckled beans, I wouldn't limit my cassoulet cooking experiences to just white beans.

Small: These varieties of beans are good in soups or simpler dishes. Like the little Basque bean I used for the Faux Cassoulet Pork & Beans, Navy beans hold their shape but are too small for my tastes for cassoulet. I want the bean to hold its own against the large pieces of sausage, duck, or other meat.

If I am traveling far from home in Gascony, I look for local varieties of bean that fit my needs: as large as my thumbnail, reasonably fresh, and locally grown. Two out of three is the rule.

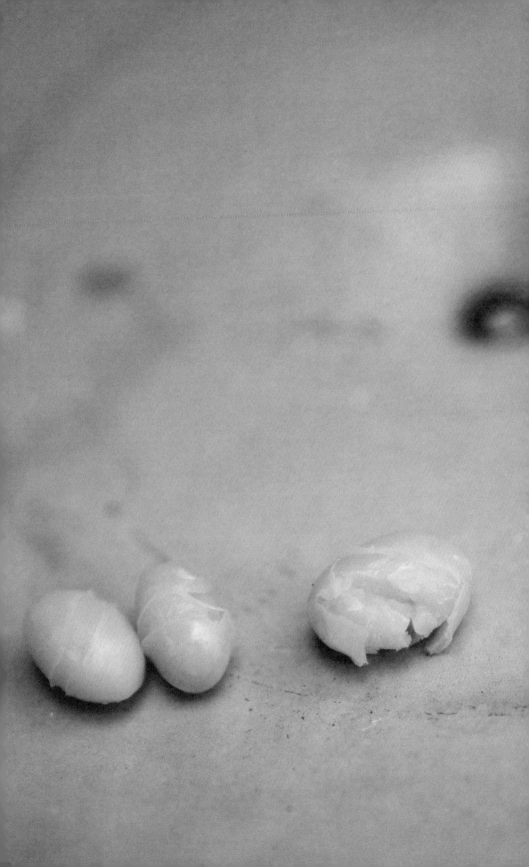

MORE ON BEANS...

SOAKING: I've been all around the internet block, consulting the latest bean wizards, scientific documents, and old fashioned cookbooks. To soak or not to soak. My conclusion is quite simple: Do whatever helps you cook more beans.

Beans that are presoaked overnight in cold water make a great cassoulet. So do beans that are quick-soaked: brought to a boil and then turned off and let sit for an hour before cooking. Even dry beans started from scratch, with no previous soaking, will catch up with an extra hour or so of cooking time. The differences, if any, are negligible and have no effect on digestibility.

COOKING: There are two important stages of making a great cassoulet: the gentle cooking of the beans in a flavorsome broth and the slow, even cooking in an oven.

The first cooking is critical. The taste of the bean must infuse the broth as much as the meat-enriched broth flavors the bean. Complex flavors, exchanged between bean and broth, are suspended in the release of pectin and starch that gradually thickens the cooking liquid. The goal is to have a perfectly balanced, earthy-tasting, rich broth that sings of bean. Too often a mean, watery broth is the culprit behind an insipid cassoulet.

Then magic happens in the oven-baking of cassoulet, when the bean and broth are placed in a wide-mouthed earthenware pot along with umami-rich charcuterie—sausage, *confit de canard*—or other roasted meat, lamb, or game. This second-stage transformation in a slow oven melds the distinct flavors of well-seasoned legumes and cured meats to transform them into cassoulet.

A LAST WORD ON SIZE: Dried beans, when fully soaked, are approximately three times their original size and approximately double their weight. I use a generous French-size portion of 100 g of dried beans per serving.

HTC: Ever try cooking some beans that just never seem to soften up? Yes, it's possible they have a "hard-to-cook" or hard-shell defect. Beans stored at too high a temperature and in too humid an environment risk forming an impenetrable shell or chemical change that affects not only the final texture or softening of the bean but its nutritive value. The best way to avoid HTC is to buy beans from a reliable source, storing them in a cool and dry environment, and using them often.

SALT THOSE BEANS: Adding salt too early may impede softening, but it is imperative to develop the taste of the beans in their broth before assembling the cassoulet. Got plenty of time? You can salt your beans earlier and let them cook slower. But even if you're in a hurry, be sure to taste and season your beans before they are finished cooking.

MYTHS...

As far as broth is concerned with the cooking of beans, I have questioned many of the cassoulet myths as I raked my sources for the essential truth. Chief among these myths is the squandering of good broth-building soaking water in the name of digestibility. Do **not** throw out the bean cooking liquid!

Next would be the myth, born out of restaurant kitchens perhaps, that inspires thrifty cooks to toss the broth's beautifully cooked vegetables into the garbage. The carrot, onions, garlic, and leeks of a great cassoulet are often strained out and discarded. Why? Because recipes say so? I beg to differ.

The last annoying bean-broth myth is that you need to add processed chicken stock or some other liquid for flavor. As you can see, we are building a beautiful broth of beans, meat and vegetables. Why would you substitute a canned product for fresh?

PORTRAIT OF MADAME BORDE, THE BEAN LADY

I see the Saturday morning market faces of the Borde family—mother and daughter—at their modest stall wonderfully laden with shallots, garlic, onions, and seasonal cabbages, spinach or potatoes. However, as I enter my busy cassoulet season, fear of bean deprivation takes over and I can't wait for Saturday. I grab Tim and we drive over to the farm of Mesdames Bordes near Francescas. It's there that Madame Borde, mother to Pauline, receives us (and other drop-by customers) into her stone barn bean sanctuary.

Last time I was there, a city slicker in a countrified outfit with a chic handbag had driven all the way from Bordeaux to buy a winter's worth of beans, Madame Borde's special "Tarbais" beans. (Technically, Tarbais beans are now defined by a protected geographic area designation, IGP Tarbais.) Here they are often called *Haricots de Mais* because—like the North American native population did—olden-days farmers planted these pole beans alongside kernels of corn so that the stalks would both support the bean vine and help replenish the soil with the bean's nitrogen fixing properties. I volunteered my own delight in having such good beans grown locally for cassoulet. The lady from the city reveled in putting me in my American outsider place by proclaiming that these beans were too good to waste on cassoulet. "These beans," she declared empirically, us only a French woman of a certain age can do, "should only be used for serving with a perfectly cooked *gigot d'agneau*—a leg of lamb."

I know how to hold my tongue, sometimes, and did. After I helped Madame De Ville load the 20 kg net bag into her smart little Peugeot and she drove off to her little city kitchen, I looked at Madame Borde. *"Oui, ils sont parfait pour un gigot,"* she said. *"Mais dans la campagne, un cassoulet faites avec mes haricots est un regal!"* ("Yes, these are perfect for a leg of lamb. But in the country, a cassoulet made with my beans is a delight!")

The Borde ladies work their family farm together with a hired couple. It requires a complex coordinated annual dance of planting fields, rotating crops, sequential harvesting, and direct sales at farm and market. This is just some of the work required to produce locally grown heritage beans. Shelling the bean pods, packing them in 500 g bags for sale, and showing up, rain or shine, at every Saturday morning market in Nerac is the work of a producer committed to selling directly to their customer.

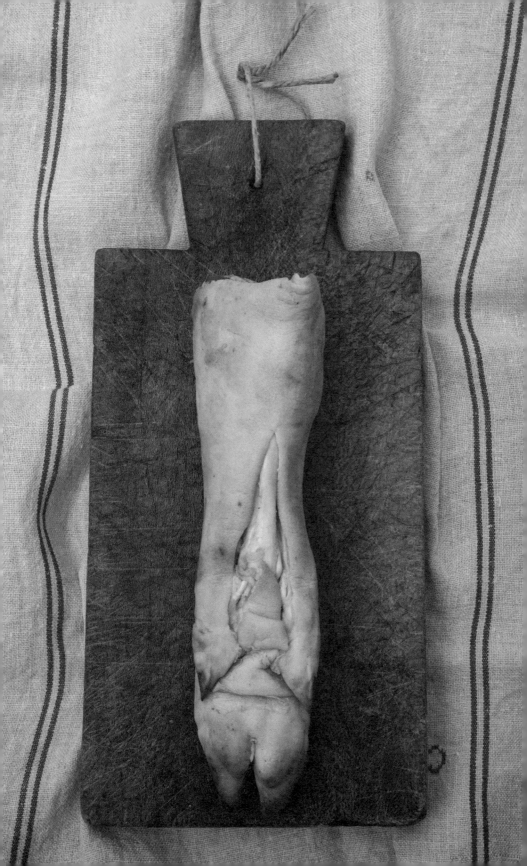

CHARCUTERIE

I was going to call this section Pork, but I realized that was simultaneously too broad and too limiting. The second essential ingredient in making a great cassoulet is more than meat. It is the subtle salty nuances of cured pork prepared in a variety of umami-loaded ways. If charcuterie is the end game of butchery, then cassoulet serves as a perfect showcase for that process of transforming meat into art.

Every cassoulet—no matter which recipe used by the rivaling *confreries* or cassoulet clubs, Michelin-starred chefs, or neighborhood cooks—all have quality charcuterie in common. Charcuterie is the French food art of transforming fresh meat, particularly pork, into a shelf-stable but flavor-enhanced version of itself. Charcuterie comes from the French words for meat or flesh *(chair)* and cooked *(cuit)*. Every part of the pig is used and falls under the charcuterie banner. Fresh shoulder meat becomes *saucisse de Toulouse*; salt-cured pork belly becomes *ventrèche*; a leg of pork is separated at the hock to become a dry-aged *jambon* or bone-in ham; thick, collagen-rich pork rind from the fatback or off the leg is rolled and tied into a neat bundle.

Good charcuterie is easier to come by these days. And with the resurgence of preserving food at home, many people are making their own delicious small goods from locally sourced pork. Besides teaching charcuterie here at Camont—I have a seemingly endless supply of bacon now—I also buy charcuterie from my farming

friends—local pig farmers, butchers and *charcutiers*—the Chapolard family of Ferme Baradieu.

Charcuterie supplies the literal backbone to the beans' cooking broth. I usually begin cooking the beans for cassoulet in an
extra-large pot half full of meaty bones: a salted or fresh *jarret*
(ham hock); a bare ham bone from a cured leg, or the end chunks
off a well-aged ham; generous, thick slices of peppery cured
ventrèche; even a short rack of confit ribs. It is the deep, savory
flavors of these salt-cured and aged meats that provide the base
notes for the fruity beans and floral herbal vegetables. If cassoulet was a perfume, it would be rich and spicy!

When you are thinking about these prime ingredients, think
hard. Good meat makes good charcuterie; good charcuterie
makes good cassoulet. Cheap meat thrown in some water will
taste foul. As chemical preservatives, additives, and artificial fla-
voring leach into the broth, it will ruin the sublime taste you are
working so hard to create.

So shop well. Buy a smaller quantity of good-quality charcuterie rather than kilos of uninteresting-tasting pig bits. A little
goes a long way.

These are the three standard charcuterie products I use for cooking the beans, making the broth, and adding to the *cassole*:

VENTRÈCHE or cured pork belly; bacon or pancetta by another name. *Ventrèche* in France tends to be lightly salted, barely smoked, if at all, and generously dusted with pepper. So using that as the criteria, a thick slab of unsmoked, salt-cured pork belly will do. Leave it in thick chunks or, if rolled, thick slices. Watch out for sugar-cured mixes or heavily smoked bacon; it's just not the taste we look for in classic cassoulet. *Ventrèche* provides the silky mouthfeel as well as that bacon flavor we all like.

JARRET OR HAM HOCK. Here I use lightly salted (in an overnight cure) or fresh hocks, unsmoked. Again, the heavy, dark-brown, smoky hocks you might use for American-style pork-and-beans are too overpowering for our more-delicate French palate. The economical hock provides bone, meat protein, collagen, and the much-valued rind to enrich the broth and provide silky mouthfeel. After cooking with the beans, the meat falls off the bone and you can add it the cassoulet.

HAM BONE AND SALT-CURED HAM ENDS. What I look for in ham is that particular French flavor, a slightly sweet saltiness that only comes from a ham that's been curing and ripening for more than a year at ambient temperatures. I am often gifted the long femur ham bone from my local charcuterie and even walked away with a prized Spanish Bellota ham bone. There was barely a tag of meat on it, but the deep flavor of that bone's broth became the base for a memorable cassoulet.

No bone? Don't worry, there are many other good pig parts you can use:

PIG'S FOOT is great for all of the above reasons but especially for that collagen-rich rind and cartilage that contribute to mouthfeel.

PIG'S EARS have no meat to speak of, but that porky rind and inner cartilage is perfect for building the bean broth. Once cooked through, the ears can be removed to fry up nice and crispy to serve on a salad.

PIG'S TAIL has its own secret—a long tail is the sign of a small-scale pork producer. Most commercially bred pigs have their tails docked at birth. A long, well-formed pig's tail for sale alongside more noble cuts like a loin roast is a good indication of an small-scale farmer and artisan butcher. Animal welfare aside, the tail, like the feet, has an abundance of cartilage and rind, plus the bonus of the marrow-rich bones at its meaty base.

COUENNE OR FRESH RIND is the uncooked and defatted skin of the pig. The fresh rind when cooked with soups, stews, and *daubes* contributes its collagen to creating the smooth mouthfeel and rich tasting sauce that binds the beans and meat together.

The charcuterie products added to the *cassole* before baking a cassoulet include:

SAUCISSE DE TOULOUSE, the authentic simple all-pork sausage, is essential in making a cassoulet. Listen up now: I am going to get pedantic. *Saucisse de Toulouse* is a pure pork meat sausage, typically 80 percent lean (from shoulder and ham meat) and 20 percent belly fat, seasoned with salt and pepper, and stuffed in a medium-size natural casing. Stop. No wine. No garlic. No sugar. No spices. Get it? The minute you start adding extra spices, flavorings, and other things you think you read on some blog, you are changing the perfect pitch of deep Southwest cooking. Yes, some people do add garlic. And someone did use wine. But in every artisan butcher shop I know and frequent in the big area around the city of Toulouse, a *saucisse de Toulouse* is exactly as I have described it.

SAUCISSE DE COUENNE literally explode with flavor in the cassoulet. I love how these succulent sausages—made with lean pork meat and cooked soft rind—taste and feel.

CONFIT DE CANARD is listed under charcuterie because it, too, is a salted and preserved meat product. *Confit de canard* is one of my favorite things to add to a cassoulet. After all, I live in "duck-duck-goose" country. However, it is not essential to make a good cassoulet, so I am giving it a special place of its own here, a simple Duck Confit primer (page 89).

LAMB, GAME, AND OTHER MEAT. As you'll see when you start looking at the 1,001 other recipes for cassoulet, this is where the recipes start to fan out and differ, accounting for taste, availability, seasonality, geography, culture, etc. Game—in the form of partridge or pheasant—rabbit, fresh pork meat, and lamb are all possible additions to a festive cassoulet. The only thing all other meat ingredients have in common is they are included for the great pleasure of the cassoulet participants. This was a dish created to accommodate everyone at the table and I am not about to turn anyone away now.

TRUC: When feeling flush, I do use some prized ham itself. Madame Grezes of Toulouse's Victor Hugo Market shared her fabulous ham tip with me so I am passing it on. She grinds an end cut of ham, about 200 g of Parma, Serrano, Bayonne, or other dry-cured country ham, and adds the ground ham to the bean cooking broth. It's magic.

MORE ON CHARCUTERIE...

Born in Carcassonne and raised in Toulouse, the great chef of the last century Prosper Montagné cemented the notions of which meat to use when he defined the Holy Trinity of Cassoulet—Carcassonne (pheasant), Toulouse (lamb), and Castelnaudary (duck). I find that as long as the essential charcuterie is used to cook the beans—whether you add duck confit to the sausage, or a tender piece of slow-cooked lamb neck and a plump game bird—and as long as you have tended your beans with care, your cassoulet will please. I have made cassoulet with nearly every barnyard fowl, from duck to guinea hen, and most other readily available meat. As long as the quality is top and chosen with the same care as the very good beans you are ennobling with meat, then you don't have to break the bank to make a very good, authentic cassoulet.

11 CHARCUTERIE

MEMBRE D'HONNEUR
GRANDE CONFRÉRIE DU CASSOULET DE CASTELNAUDARY
· 2011 ·

En passant par Castelnaudary
Ne manquez pas de vous régaler
Et dégustez notre cassoulet
Bien apprécié de tous les maris,
Parents, amis, d'ici et d'ailleurs
Car on le dit parmi les meilleurs
Et pourquoi pas repartir confits gras
Qui lui aussi vous enchantera.

L'équipe de fabrication
vous propose un choix varié
de terrines et de corbeilles-cadeaux
à l'intérieur.

PORTRAIT OF THE CHAPOLARD FAMILY

When I first met Christiane and Dominique Chapolard at a small farmers' market, I had no idea that our lives would become so deeply entwined. How did I end up spending long hours in a refrigerated butchering room, traipsing around a muddy Gascon farm looking at newborn piglets, and bumping along behind a truck fill of slaughtered pigs down a country road at dawn?

My journey to learn about charcuterie was aided and enabled by the Chapolard family's commitment to producing great farmstead charcuterie, as well as sharing their farm-based *savoir-faire*. The key to this commitment, this seed-to-sausage philosophy, is time.

Dominique Chapolard, whose frosted mustache bends into smile, explains the seasonal points of their family farming business philosophy: "From spring seed to fall harvest is 6 to 8 months; from farrowing to weaning to fattening to slaughter is another 16 months. Add a week in the butcher and 4 to 8 weeks of curing; now our 'seed' is indeed 'sausage' and 4 days a week we deliver it into customers' market baskets. Add all that up and it's a 2-year investment before we see any of the €9 a kilo ($4.50 a pound) that we are paid—the average of our artisan products."

Like other producers I know, the Chapolards have become more than my favorite merchants. They are my teachers and some of my closest friends. I shop, work, and socialize with them throughout the year, so writing about them is like writing a little love letter. Describing them as a robust and handsome family that works and plays hard is a simplistic way to say they have a huge appetite for life.

Can you imagine starting work at 6 a.m., before a breakfast break, then finishing the work day at 7 p.m. before a rousing game of Ultimate Frisbee at a local high school gym with a group of multi-generational friends? Or swapping out your white rubber boots from the cutting room for a pair of wooden clogs to learn Gascon folk dancing? The Chapolards' commitment is to their community and quality of life—including their high-quality charcuterie products.

Time: It's all about taking the time to do something well. The Chapolard pigs are slaughtered after a well-cared-for 12-month life, weighing in at 180 to 200 kg (350 to 440 lbs). The meat is complex in flavor and deeply colored—pork is red meat—and has the mature cell structure needed to produce excellent dry-cured products.

Jacques Chapolard oversees the breeding program for the family farm—Ferme Baradieu—working with agricultural experts to create a closed-circle production where everything is raised and grown on the same farm. Cradling a piglet in his arms, he explains that—unlike pork rushed to fit an industrial standard with the pig slaughtered at 5 or 6 months—Baradieu's 12-month-old Large White/Duroc/Landrace pigs grow fully developed skeletons to support the muscle meat we ultimately eat as chops, roasts, and bacon. They are fed on farm-grown grains and cereals, a balanced diet that produces balanced meat, satisfying to the palate and tooth.

When pork is allowed to fully develop, the resulting texture and taste supports a diverse range of cooking techniques. This same pork is destined for charcuterie: Curing by salting, brining, and air drying. Imagine trying to dry veal rather than beef. Or only eating yogurt instead of 18-month Roquefort cheese! If the Chapolards could produce quality charcuterie in half the time, they would—what farmer wouldn't? Instead, they take the time to produce good pigs so that their products will be delicious and healthy, which also allows them to maintain a sustainable family farm.

The old farm buildings at Baradieu wear their history well and support the continuing tradition that this dedicated family upholds. The Chapolards' farmstead charcuterie stands apart for its excellence, and I am happy to use it as a base for my Classic Cassoulet.

Merci to the whole family: Dominique, Christiane, Jacques, Bruno, Marc, and Cécile!

SEASONINGS

An ensemble of fresh vegetables, spices, and herbs infuse the initial bean broth when making cassoulet. These unsung vegetarian heroes support the sexy charcuterie and fancy beans with a base of complex flavors. Building this broth is the true secret behind a great cassoulet. In the oven's gentle heat, the well-seasoned soup is eventually absorbed by the beans and reduced in the open pot, condensing the remaining liquid into a rich, delicious but loosely textured sauce.

So what makes this sauce taste so good?

Of course, it begins with the beans, cooked in a broth of their own making, with water alone—no added stock needed. Just as when making a wonderful vegetable soup, I choose my ingredients carefully. I love this part of making cassoulet and I think this is where good cooks really shine. Much like making jams, bean-making is hard to do in huge batches. The goal is a perfect pot of beans cradled in just enough broth. You can accomplish this in three easy steps.

STEP ONE: THE WATER

Good water is essential to any cassoulet recipe. Two qualities of water affect cooking beans for cassoulet: hardness (or mineral content) and taste.

Some experts say water that's high in calcium and magnesium will require longer bean-cooking time. Although my tap water here in the Garonne Valley is rich in calcium, I have never discerned any problem. Perhaps that's because I am used to my presoaked beans needing 45 minutes to an hour to cook, and I don't try to rush. It's important to learn to taste for doneness with each batch, not to rely only on a timer.

The taste of your cooking water is also critical. Would you drink your tap water straight from the faucet? I do here at Camont. It tastes great and I don't need to recycle plastic water bottles. However, I have visited areas where the smell of chlorine from the kitchen faucet is so strong that I wouldn't consider drinking or cooking with it. In these places, I use bottled water.

If you presoak the beans overnight or use the quick-soak method (see page 56), I advise you to cherish the first bean liquor: its soaking water. I don't toss the soaking liquid. If it's good enough for Harold McGee—American's best-known food science authority—and Steve Sando of Rancho Gordo, it's good enough for me.

Good water is the foundation for your broth and the soaking water is perfectly good to begin cooking your cassoulet beans.

STEP TWO:
THE VEGETABLES

Fat soup carrots are full of sweet flavor that complements the beans. If you watch me work, I almost always add a peeled, whole carrot to the broth first so it can cook fully and release its flavor. Leaving the carrot whole lets it cook slowly and maintain its nutrients better, but it also gives me the flexibility to use it as I want to without wasting it. Sometimes I fish it out of the beans, douse it with salt and pepper, and eat it as a snack. If I'm not hungry, I might give it to the dog as a treat. More likely, I'll cut it into bean-size pieces and add it back to the cassoulet.

A **pungent onion** is important for two reasons: It provides a slow-releasing, sweet flavor, and it holds the spices. I peel the onion, leave it whole, and stud it with whole cloves so they don't get lost in the broth and end up under someone's tooth.

Garlic, used in moderation, flavors the broth and beans without overpowering it. I use just a few whole garlic cloves in my broth.

STEP THREE:
THE HERBS & SPICES

Besides the few **cloves** studded into the onion, I add the following ingredients to the broth as it starts to cook.

I grow **thyme, bay laurel,** and **lovage** in my *potager* or kitchen garden, and use them widely in my Gascon cooking. They are the trilogy of herbal flavors that perfume most of the soups and stews I cook at Camont. Thyme is the base note and adds its strength to the broth; bay laurel is common to most soups and imparts roundness to taste of the broth; lovage smells and tastes like celery but with a bit more oomph. Thyme, bay, and lovage not only flavor the bean broth, they also retain some of their substantial medicinal value, including digestive and antiseptic properties. I love the garden flavor they infuse into the broth but I think they also must add to the ultimate healthfulness of the whole cassoulet.

Sea salt is added when the beans have opened up to the idea of being salted. I know that sounds a bit pretentious, but consider that the beans needs to hydrate and cook, and then release their starch, before being open to accepting the salt. Adding salt too early to the broth impedes the softening process.

Whole **black peppercorns** are the spicy complement to the sweeter flavors bubbling away by now.

Certainly these are all very basic ingredients. But if the carrots are too old, the onions flat-tasting, the dried herbs old and dusty, how can you expect your beans to taste great? Choose carefully and shop well.

DUCK CONFIT IN ONE, TWO, THREE

1. BUY A WHOLE DUCK & CUT INTO PARTS
2. SALT & LEAVE OVERNIGHT
3. COOK SLOWLY IN FAT & STORE

Confit de canard is charcuterie of the highest order, transforming fresh duck meat into a more elegant and silky version of itself. In short, confit (from the French verb *confire*, to preserve) is the act of conserving meat in fat—traditionally duck, goose, or pork—using salt and heat to create a shelf-stable product. Considered a luxury item now by many, *confit de canard* is a pantry staple in most Southwest France households, bistros, and restaurants. Seasonally, one makes it at home (as described below) between November and March, or buys it year-round in cans or jars at supermarkets, farmers' markets, or butcher shops. *Confit de canard* is also readily available by mail order from online sources internationally. There are more than 8,000 listings on "where to find *confit de canard*" on Google!

However, if you want to make your own confit—whether for use in cassoulet, in other dishes, or to enjoy on its own—this brief tutorial should make it approachable and easy in your own home kitchen.

Note: In France, a proper fatted duck will be raised for 14 to 16 weeks and then fattened on whole corn for 11 to 14 days. This fattening process produces a big duck weighing 6 to 7 kilos. My instructions are for preparing traditional *confit de canard* with a mature fatted duck weighing 6-plus-kilos (13-plus-pounds). The fatted duck carcass will yield enough fat to render the confit. But if working with smaller, leaner, and younger ducks, you can buy additional duck fat. Expect to use around 2 to 4 cups of duck fat for each duck.

STEP 1: BEGIN WITH A WHOLE DUCK

1. Cut the duck into pieces: Two legs, two breasts removed from the carcass, two wings, and the neck.

2. You can also confit the gizzard, heart, and liver, and reserve the rest of the carcass for making rillettes.

3. Trim off excess skin and fat; reserve for rendering.

4. To render the fat: Chop all fat and skin into small cubes the size of dice. Place in a large saucepan with a half a glass of water (about 4 fl oz) and cook slowly over low heat until all the fat has melted. Remove the skin and cracklings and crisp them up in a separate pan if you like. They are great seasoned with salt and pepper and eaten like popcorn. The liquid fat remaining should be clear and light gold in color. How much fat you have will depend on how your ducks were raised (see Note, page 89).

STEP 2: SALT THE MEAT

1. Rub the salt onto all the pieces. Use 1 tablespoon coarse salt per piece of duck, or about 200 g for the whole duck.

2. Place the salted pieces in a bowl or on a tray with raised edges. Cover with a tea towel and leave about 12 hours in the refrigerator or in a very cold room.

3. When ready to cook, wipe off excess salt with a dry cloth or paper towel.

STEP 3: COOK SLOWLY IN FAT & STORE

1. Put rendered duck fat (you will need 2 to 4 cups) into a deep pot and bring it to a simmer; do not let the fat come to a boil. Add the duck meat to the simmering fat, a couple pieces at a time, letting it return to a simmer after each addition to help the fat stay at a constant temperature.

2. Cook very slowly until done, about 1.5 to 2 hours. The meat juices will run clear and a wooden skewer will easily pierce the meat.

3. Remove the duck from the fat and place into containers. Cover with liquid duck fat; store and let ripen before using. (See TRUC, below.)

In the era before refrigeration, confit was stored in glazed terracotta pots, covered with fat, sealed with brown paper and string, then stored at cellar temperature.

Today, people freeze confit very successfully. Like most of my neighbors, I stick to the canning method, carefully sealing my confit and fat in glass jars and processing in a boiling water bath for 1.5 to 2 hours. You can also store confit in a covered container in the refrigerator for several weeks to a few months. In that case, it is important that the entire pieces of meat, including any bones, are sealed by the fat.

TRUC: *Although traditional confit is best when allowed to ripen and rest for several weeks after preparation, it's possible to consume it sooner. If that's your plan, cook the confit slower and longer—a minimum of 2 hours at very low temperatures, until it is almost falling off the bone. However, here in Gascony, we take the time to prepare winter goods in advance.*

PORTRAIT OF
JEHANNE RIGNAULT

I love this photo of Jehanne Rignault in front of a backdrop of golden straw with a hefty bundle of moulard duck in her arms. She is the embodiment of all things *canard* for me here in Southwest France, and a strong example of an artisan producer who creates a selection of impressive products from the ground up. She also makes some of the best *confit de canard* in the area and I have watched her like a duck-loving hawk for years, learning some of her secrets.

Recently retired, Jehanne has been a farmer, a cook, and an innkeeper for more than 30 years. She also is a *charcuterière*—someone who preserves meat (in her case, mostly duck). She has taught me how she tends to her flocks, from the first cheeping handfuls of down that arrive a day old on the farm, to 7 kg mature beasts. Duck, in all its glory, is the delicious aim of the Ferme de Boué.

In addition to raising a couple thousand ducks and processing them into *confit, magret seché* (like duck prosciutto), rillettes, and paté to sell at local markets, Jehanne created one of the first Ferme Auberges, places where city folks can experience and eat the food that is produced on a single farm.

When friends arrive for the first time in Gascony, I love to take them to Jehanne's wonderful family farm restaurant. On weekends and summer days, Jehanne would reign over a sumptuous meal served in an airy hall built in the old stables, explaining each course along the way. Prepared by Jehanne and her friendly crew, a Sunday lunch on the farm was an edible tour of her commitment to growing good food: duck, veal, carrots, potatoes, salad, bread, and strawberries.

Meeting Jehanne in her element, surrounded by the land she has tended for three decades, is a reminder of how much dedication goes into creating any one element of our delicious cassoulets. She keeps a farmer's pragmatic eye on her feathered charges, raising them carefully in the traditional way— first fed on pasture, then finished on whole corn—before harvesting the rich, red meat for conserving.

Once salted, cooked, and preserved, Jehanne's products serve as the basis for many a good Gascon meal. The Ferme de Boué has now passed into a newer generation's hands, and the tradition of Jehanne's carefully crafted duck charcuterie lives on as I teach my own students how to make duck confit here at Camont.

RECIPES

CLASSIC CASSOULET

By definition, cassoulet is simply beans and meat cooked together in an open vessel in an oven. The mysterious alchemy of flavors and textures develops during slow cooking. I adopted this recipe as the gold standard after years of eating and making cassoulet in the heartland of the Lauragais Plain in Southwest France. It's the best of all the best cassoulet I have ever eaten.

It is essential cassoulet: basic, bonafide, easy to prepare, authentic, traditional, and real. I have prepared, taught, cooked, and eaten this version of cassoulet in kitchens around the world.

And, in the tradition of kitchen alchemy, I've added my own trucs *(or tricks) to elevate the basic and simple ingredients into a new gold standard—the golden, starchy crust concealing a molten heart of beany goodness.*

The real secret is the careful combining of very good ingredients, slow cooking, and wholehearted enjoyment. Here, I use the classic Southwestern French charcuterie meats: saucisse de Toulouse *(a lean, all-pork sausage),* ventrèche *(salt-cured pork belly),* couenne *(pork rind), and* confit de canard *(preserved duck). This is not gospel, but it's pretty close. See the descriptions of the ingredients in the previous section to understand how each plays a critical role.*

As much a state of mind as a recipe, making this Classic Cassoulet should feed your spirit as well as your belly. Invite a few friends and make it a fête! *That's what cassoulet is about.*

QUANTITY: This makes an extra-large cassoulet that fills a 4-liter (4-quart) *cassole* or deep baking dish and feeds 10 people easily.

TIMING: Preparation and cooking takes 1.5 hours, followed by 3 hours baking time, with minimal interference by the cook.

TOTAL TIME: 5 hours.

You can start making a cassoulet in the afternoon, using presoaked or fresh beans, and serve it for dinner that evening. If you forgot to soak the beans ahead, you can use the quick-soak method (page 56) and add another 2 hours to the total preparation and cooking time. If you have never made a cassoulet, or are not an experienced cook, add some extra time to allow for learning along the way.

THE FOUR SIMPLE STEPS TO CASSOULET

I have organized the cooking into four parts:

1. Cooking the beans
2. Preparing the meat
3. Building the cassoulet
4. Cooking and serving the cassoulet.

If needed, you can prepare the beans one day and then assemble, bake, and serve on another. A cassoulet will even hold well in the refrigerator once fully cooked and can be slowly reheated the following day.

Before beginning, make sure to read the previous chapters describing the ingredients you will be using.

COOKING THE BEANS

INGREDIENTS:

1 kg (2.2 lb) dried white beans
rehydrated by soaking several hours in water, or bringing to a boil and letting sit one hour

1 carrot
peeled and left whole

1 onion
peeled and left whole

4 whole cloves
studded into the onion

2 to 4 large garlic cloves
unpeeled

1 bouquet garni
made of several bay leaves, celery or lovage leaves, parsley stalks, and fresh or dried thyme, tied with string or placed in cheesecloth bag

1 tsp black peppercorns
whole or cracked

3 cm (about 1 in) thick slice of ventrèche, pancetta, or salt pork

1 ham hock, ham bone, or pigs foot

100 g fresh pork rind (couenne)
about a 4x12-inch strip, rolled and tied with a string

1. Place all of the ingredients in a large stock pot. Cover with 2 to 3 liters (2 to 3 quarts) of good-tasting water. **Do not** add salt; the seasoning can be adjusted when building the cassoulet.

2. Bring the pot to a boil. Reduce the heat and simmer gently for 45 to 60 minutes or until both beans and broth are done: The beans will be cooked and barely tender, their skins will turn papery and begin to collapse. The cooking liquid will look milky, not clear, and taste delicious enough to eat immediately.

3. Remove from heat and set aside.

PREPARING THE MEAT

INGREDIENTS:

confit de canard
*10 preserved duck wings (the
manchons or wing drumettes),
or 5 preserved duck legs*

*A leg from a fatted duck, known as a
canard gras, can easily weigh nearly
a pound each, so adjust accordingly*

saucisse de Toulouse
*about 1 kg (2 lb) total,
or one link per person*

*You can prepare the meat while the beans are cooking. This is where
you can be flexible using fresh sausage, preserved duck or goose, ham or
cured pork, lamb shanks, etc.*

1. Prepare the confit duck by scraping off most of the softened fat from
the surface. If using larger legs, cut through the joint, separating the thigh
from the drumstick. This results in a neat little package of confit meat that
is easier to assemble and, later, to serve on the plate.

2. In a skillet, brown the duck, skin side only. Add the sausages to the pan
and brown on all sides. (You don't need to fully cook them at this stage.
They will continue to cook in the cassoulet and give their juices to the
beans and broth.)

TRUC: If you can buy saucisse de Toulouse *in one long link, make a pretty
spiral and brown on each side.*

BUILDING THE CASSOULET

The traditional *cassole* dish has a bottom just half of the diameter as the top, making a deep, slant-sided glazed terracotta pot. There is no need to line the pot with fat or rind.

Remove the beans from the heat and then remove all the meat and seasonings: the bouquet garni, onion, carrot, and cooked rind, hock, and pork belly, and any bones.

Slice the *ventrèche* into thick slabs and set aside to use when assembling the cassoulet. Chop the onion, carrot, and rind into small bean-size pieces and return to the beans, along with any ham or hock meat. Gently stir together without breaking up the beans.

Taste and adjust the seasoning of the broth and the beans. You can add a little salt—but remember the confit and sausage will add salt, too—some more black pepper and pinch of *piment d'esplette,* if you like. This seasoned bean stock is savory, delicious, and silky on the mouth.

Using a large slotted spoon or ladle, transfer enough beans to make a thick layer into your *cassole* or dish. Add the confit in a second layer, then add another layer of beans. Place the sausage on top, then finish with the final layer of beans. I like to stud the top of the cassoulet with slabs of pork belly so they slowly baste the top crust and get crackling crisp.

Add just enough bean stock to the full *cassole* to barely cover the beans. Any remaining broth should be saved for basting, if needed, or making bean soup with leftovers.

COOKING THE CASSOULET

Heat the oven to 150°C (300°F). Slip the *cassole* into the hot oven and let the cassoulet bake, slowly, as long as you can, approximately 3 hours. A cassoulet baked in an electric oven is certainly browned in 1.5 to 2 hours, but letting it ripen slowly for 3 hours is my favorite way.

Once baked, I break the crust by pushing it down with a large spoon into the juices, two or three times, as needed. Early on, when it is still very soupy, I baste the top beans with the broth and encourage the juices to mingle. Slowly, a wonderful crust of beans, starch, rind, and fat forms during cooking so there is no need for that offensive sprinkle of breadcrumbs. The beans and starchy sauce make the perfect topping without any assistance.

By the time the cassoulet is baked, the surface will be dry and crisp; a perfectly golden bean crust will have formed. I like to see the molten broth burbling up through the beans and running right to the edges.

When done, serve straight from oven to table. Sit down with your friends and enjoy!

TRUC: For me, breadcrumbs are reserved for canned or store-bought cassoulet needing a quick fix in a very hot oven. I never use them on homemade cassoulet. Although I love anything gratiné, I do think it's a disservice to the beans to cover up all their hard work. You can have it both ways and save the breadcrumbs for the leftovers!

A WORD ON TIME,
THE HIDDEN INGREDIENT

Cassoulet is perfectly done baking, low and slow, in about 3 hours. However, I have been known to crank the heat up to 250°C (475°F) and push the time to a quick 1.5 hours when my schedule requires it. And it works. So why go slow?

There is a magic that happens as the bean starch and meat proteins bind slowly in the herb-scented broth. As I get older, I find I am more patient. Even with a slow 3-hour bake, if I start preparing the cassoulet from the soaked bean stage at around 3 p.m. I'll be ready for dinner at 8!

Some prep can be done in advance—all or in part—by cooking the beans ahead, or assembling before baking. But whipping out a huge beautiful bowl of bubbling cassoulet before my guests' eyes is part of the show. So, time yourself from the dinner bell and work backwards.

TO SERVE A CASSOULET

Pour a glass of rustic French red wine, like a Madiran, Cahors, something from the Minervois, or another Languedoc regional wine.

Bring the cassoulet to the table in its piping-hot *cassole* and break the final crust while everyone enjoys a glass of wine. Spoon the steaming cassoulet into dishes, distributing the confit, sausage, bacon, and crusty bits evenly.

Raise a toast "to those who showed up!" and begin the round of tall tales and food stories as the dishes are passed around the kitchen table well into the dark winter night.

ALL-DUCK CASSOULET

Duck confit is one of my favorite ingredients to add to a classic cassoulet. It helps define and succinctly impart the flavor of Southwest France. I always have some in my pantry as I make duck confit from fat French ducks several times a winter. That's part of living in Gascony.

I wanted to make a pork-free, all-duck cassoulet to see how the flavors of duck charcuterie—confit, sausage, and duck bacon—would work on their own. But, if making or buying duck confit is difficult for you, why not just start with a whole fresh or frozen duck? That's what we did here to make this silky-smooth and creamy cassoulet using just fresh duck. I added an abundant amount of garlic, and kept the other seasonings to a minimum to let that golden duck flavor shine through.

QUANTITY: Serves 8 easily.

TIMING: You can prepare the roast duck and beans at the same time, or separately, and assemble for final cooking. It's best to let the salted duck rest overnight. The duck is cooked in 2 hours (while the beans cook); building the cassoulet takes less than 30 minutes. Then the final bake takes an additional 2 hours.

TOTAL TIME: 4.5 hours.

COOKING THE DUCK

INGREDIENTS:

whole roasting duck
2 kg (4.5 lb)

coarse sea salt

2 large serving spoons
duck fat

1 head of garlic
broken into cloves, unpeeled

2 to 3 bay leaves
fresh or dried

1 tsp black peppercorns
whole or cracked

1. Prepare the duck by salting generously inside the cavity and all over the skin. Chill overnight, or for several hours, in the refrigerator.

2. Heat the oven to 150°C (300°F). Knock excess salt off the duck. Place the duck and duck fat in the bottom of a cast-iron pot that has a tight-fitting lid.

3. Add garlic, bay leaves, and peppercorns, pushing the garlic down into the duck fat.

4. Cover the pot. Place in the heated oven and let the duck cook in its own juices and fat until tender, about 2 hours. (The duck is well cooked when easily pierced with a skewer or knife point.)

5. Remove the duck from the liquid and set aside to cool.

6. Strain fat and juices and let them separate. Pour off fat for later use; keep the remaining juices to add to the cassoulet.

7. Remove the breast and legs from the duck carcass. Cut the meat into serving portions and discard the carcass (or save for broth). Peel garlic and reserve for use in the cassoulet.

COOKING THE BEANS

INGREDIENTS:

800 g dried large
white beans, such as Lingot
*rehydrated by soaking several hours
in water, or bringing to a boil and
letting sit one hour*

1 carrot
peeled and left whole

2 large leeks
cleaned and chopped

1 tsp black peppercorns
whole or crushed

duck wings and neck

bouquet garni
*made of several bay leaves, celery or
lovage leaves, parsley stalks, and fresh
or dried thyme, tied with string or
placed in cheesecloth bag*

*You can prepare the beans at the same time as the duck, then let them rest
until you're ready to assemble the cassoulet.*

1. Place all of the ingredients in a large stock pot. Cover with 2 liters
(2 quarts) of good-tasting water. **Do not** add salt; the seasoning can be
adjusted when building the cassoulet.

2. Bring the pot to a boil. Reduce heat and simmer gently for 45 to 60
minutes or until both beans and broth are done: The beans will be cooked
and barely tender, their skins will turn papery and begin to collapse. The
cooking liquid will look milky, not clear, and taste delicious enough to eat
immediately.

3. Remove from heat and set aside.

BUILDING THE CASSOULET

For this cassoulet, I use a wide glazed terracotta pot about 10 cm (4 in) deep.

First, taste the broth and beans and adjust the seasoning. This is a slightly sweeter broth than the classic version, as both the Lingots and the leeks have a gentle flavor. Use just enough salt to balance. Remember you will be adding the deep-flavored duck juices and confit garlic, too.

Using a large slotted spoon, place the beans in your *cassole* to make a thick base. Nestle the duck pieces into the beans. Add the cooked garlic by squeezing the now-soft cloves out of their paper skins.

Add just enough bean stock to barely cover the beans, leaving the duck meat standing above the liquid. Drizzle the defatted duck juices over the top for a rich *demi-glace* topping.

COOKING THE CASSOULET

Heat the oven to 175°C (350°F). Bake the cassoulet slowly for about 2 hours.

The magic of this cassoulet is that the bean broth and duck fat emulsifies into a pale, bubbling, smooth, garlicky sauce as the duck skin browns.

When golden brown and very hot, serve this cassoulet straight from oven to table. A winter endive salad dressed with walnuts and walnut oil is the perfect accompaniment.

FAUX CASSOULET: SIMPLE PORK & BEANS

Hungry for beans and pork, but not in the mood for a French dance of cassoulet? This is what I do when I'm not up for cooking a full-blown Classic Cassoulet. I start cooking dried beans, add anything vegetable and herbal lying around, and toss in a few sausages and good bacon at the end. Eh voilà! My French version of Pork & Beans, a simple supper that stands up to a bottle of local wine.

It's too simple, too delicious. And it takes just about 5 real minutes of chopping, plus a couple of hours of cooking. That's not much more than the time it takes to run out to the store or order a mediocre takeout meal. While the beans are cooking, you can read a book, take a walk, or just watch the leaves drop from the trees. And you don't even need a can opener.

It's not really cassoulet, but it is very tasty. And the next day there are leftovers for lunch along with an egg poached the bean liquor. Remember: buy good beans, use good water, kiss your butcher, pay attention. That's what makes the difference!

QUANTITY: Serves 4.

TIMING: From start to finish, dried beans to supper, this is an easy one. Begin cooking and a little over 2 hours later, supper is served.

TOTAL TIME: Just over 2 hours.

INGREDIENTS:

500 g (1 lb) dried
small beans
Navy or similar

1 large carrot
peeled and left whole

1 large onion
peeled and left whole

2 shallots
peeled and left whole

2 garlic cloves
peeled and left whole

1 tsp black peppercorns
whole

handful of ham ends
*plus some good bones or a hock,
salted or not*

1 bouquet garni
*made of several bay leaves, celery or
lovage leaves, parsley stalks, and fresh
or dried thyme, tied with string or
placed in cheesecloth bag*

4 slices bacon
thickly sliced

fresh sausage
1 per person

1. In a large saucepan over high heat, cover the dry beans with three times their volume of water and bring to a boil. Reduce heat to medium and let simmer. The beans will soak, soften, and cook at the same time. Once the beans have tripled in size and are no longer wrinkled, control the water level, making sure the beans remain submerged. Once the beans have finished soaking, you only need enough water to cover beans by about 5 cm (2 in).

2. Add the vegetables and any ham ends or bones. Cover, let come to a boil, then reduce heat and simmer until the beans are tender, about 45 to 50 minutes more. Taste and add salt as desired.

3. When the beans are tender, remove the carrot, celery, onion, garlic, and ham bones. Dice the cooked vegetables and return to the pot; simmer to combine the flavors. Discard the ham bones.

4. When the beans are almost done cooking, fry some good thick pieces of bacon and a few sausages. Once browned, add the sausages to the pot. Serve the beans topped with the crisped bacon pieces.

SUMMER CASSOULET

My idea for a summer cassoulet began with the arrival of the first rare fresh shelling beans, called Coco de Pamiers, one late summer. A wonderful tasting and creamy French bean, they come from the rich river valley at Pamiers in the Ariege area, south of the Lauragais Plain. I wanted to create something light to celebrate this bean. My summer cassoulet is more a soup than a stew, but it still begins with the bean!

I buy Coco beans in a 10 kg net bag. I freeze them fresh or grow them up long poles in my potager and harvest a handful at a time. They have a plump, creamy texture and hold their shape when cooked. Their fruitiness marries well with other summer vegetables straight from the market or garden: tomatoes, leeks, zucchini, onion. What better way to celebrate the first harvest than to make a light summer soup enriched with these pillows of nutritional goodness!

For more about the Coco, see Beans, page 49.

QUANTITY: Serves 8.

TOTAL TIME: 1.5 hours.

INGREDIENTS:

500 g (1 lb) fresh Coco beans
shelled

1 leek
trimmed, cleaned, and cut into rounds

2 garlic cloves
peeled and left whole

3 cm (about 1 in) thick slice
of ventrèche

coarse sea salt & freshly
ground black pepper

piment d'espelette

8 small carrots
cut into bean-size dice

8 zucchini
cut into bean-size dice

2 to 4 tomatoes
*very ripe; leave skin on and dice to
same size as other vegetables*

1. After removing the fresh beans from their pod, rinse and place in large lidded pot. Cover with 2 to 3 liters (2 to 3 quarts) of good-tasting water. **Do not** add salt; the seasoning can be adjusted after the beans are cooked.

2. Add the leek, garlic, and ventrèche. Cover and cook over low heat until the beans are tender. At a slow simmer, fresh beans can take anywhere from 25 to 45 minutes.

3. Season the broth with salt, pepper, and *piment d'espelette*. Add the rest of the vegetables and simmer for 5 minutes more.

4. Remove the ventrèche from the soup, slice thinly and use to garnish each bowl. Alternately, you can add some thin slices of *jambon de Campagne* or other air-dried ham.

5. Serve with a good baguette, a fresh green salad, and glasses of ice-cold rosé wine.

GARBURE

Consider garbure as the Gascon lagniappe, *that little something extra that a shopkeeper gives a good customer. Garbure can be made on its own or it can be the perfect use for leftovers after making a good and generous cassoulet. (I always seem to have a few beans left in my* cassole *at the end of a good cassoulet, so it's a perfect place to begin a quick version of this classic Béarnaise dish.) Or just toss some soaked or fresh beans in the broth as it starts to cook; the beans will be done by the time your garbure is done.*

Garbure is neither soup nor stew and not baked in an oven. But it shares the same elements of a cassoulet, with the addition of some more vegetables: turnips, leeks, potatoes, and a curly green Savoy cabbage. More vegetable than meat, this warming, thick soup gets a leg of confit stirred in at the end to enrich the broth. Serve garbure in a wide soup plate over a slice of rustic bread that has been rubbed with garlic. It will transport you straight to your grandmother's kitchen... that is, if your grandmother lives in Southwest France.

QUANTITY: Serves 6.

TIMING: 30 minutes to chop and prepare; 1.5 hours to cook.

TOTAL TIME: 2 hours.

INGREDIENTS:

400 g (14 oz)
ventrèche demi-sel*
cut into large chunks, about
3 cm (1 in) wide

2 leeks
cut into knuckle-size pieces

2 carrots
peeled and cut into big chunks

2 onions
peeled and coarsely chopped

2 turnips
peeled and chopped

4 garlic cloves
peeled and chopped

100 g (4 oz) dried white beans
soaked overnight

1 bouquet garni
made of several bay leaves, celery
or lovage leaves, parsley stalks, and
fresh or dried thyme, tied with string
or placed in cheesecloth bag

coarse sea salt & whole black
peppercorns

4 large potatoes
peeled and cubed

1 savoy cabbage
cored, halved, and cut into strips

confit de canard
1 leg or a couple of wings,
with some duck fat

bread
pain de campagne or other rustic loaf;
1 thick slice per serving

grating cheese (optional)

1. Place the ventrèche, leeks, carrots, onions, turnips, garlic, and beans in a lidded soup pot and cover with 2 liters (2 quarts) of fresh water. Add the bouquet garni, a spoonful of salt, and a dozen peppercorns.

2. Cover, place over high heat, and bring to a boil. Reduce heat and simmer for about 1 hour.

3. Add the potatoes and cabbage; cook 45 minutes more.

4. Add the *confit de canard* and a little of the duck fat and continue cooking for 10 minutes.

5. Toast the bread, if you like, and place each slice in a wide bowl or soup plate. Remove the ventrèche and confit from the soup and serve on a hot plate. Ladle the soup over the bread and pass the meat at the table. Alternately, you can place all the bread in a wide oven-proof bowl; ladle the soup and vegetables over it, sprinkle it with a hard grating cheese place in a hot oven until brown. Serve immediately.

* Fresh pork belly that has been salted for about 2 hours before using; alternately you can use just fresh pork belly, cured bacon, ham hock, or ends of ham.

THE KITCHEN-AT-CAMONT

What my Kitchen-at-Camont lacks in modern gadgets, organization, and space, it makes up in charm. French eighteenth-century charm exudes from the walls made of porous stone and brick, the uneven and fractured red tiles, and the *brocante* (vintage) shop inventory of terrines, graters, whisks, and pottery. Yes, it looks a bit like the quintessential TV set—and it has been, in the BBC "French Odyssey" series, as well as the photo set for most of my blog and website pictures over the years (and the kitchen photos shot for this book).

But I remember, first, the bare-plastered walls and the collapsed roof rubble, a solitary tree reaching toward the open sky, long before we shoveled and emptied, scraped, cleaned, and reroofed the kitchen. The nearly square space seemed enormous then. Twenty square meters (about 200 square feet) of open plan nicely crowds 20 years of cooking *poule-au-pot, confit de canard,* and cassoulet into a memorable space. Before there was electricity or running water, I had cooked dinners for 25 guests, thrown several parties, and hosted a wedding. I began to define *ma cuisine*—my cooking—by the four walls that defined *la cuisine*—my kitchen.

The original farm, Camont, was a sprawling several hundred acres along the riverbanks of the Garonne. More than 150 years ago as the Canal de Deux Mers was built, bisecting the fields with an arrow-straight modern waterway, the old *pigeonnier* served as a *relais,* or waystation, where bargemen, hauling their goods to Toulouse or Bordeaux, would stop to rest horses and spirits. Camont was a convenient overnight stop before the difficult Garonne River locks; I can imagine the many meals cooked over the two-meter open fireplace. Now, the Kitchen-at-Camont sits amid just 2.5 acres of unruly canalside gardens. It is school room, office, and stage for my kitchen chronicles, the place where I have taught and entertained guests and students these last 20 years.

After getting the roof on, and adding a little plumbing and some electricity, I made some small but significant improvements to the functionality of this 300-year-old farmhouse. It was fine for a long while, as it was.

Then, in 2015, when my sister Stephanie came to join me, we raised the comfort level a couple notches and began Phase Two at Camont. We added an ivory enamel woodstove tucked into the open fireplace. Although I no longer cook on the open fire, the bean pot fits nicely on the stove and it heats the old stone walls more efficiently. Summer is always easy living outside, but as Camont becomes our year-round home, we are extending our reach for winter. A giant new refrigerator lurks under the hand-hewn ashwood staircase; my library of cookbooks climbs these stairs, alternating reference sources with the wall-mounted iPad. I love where the brand-new and the very old intersect.

Even as I write, there is a small, strong team of Polish stonemasons restoring the barn next door—the future Keeping Kitchen—and I look forward to more pantry space where jars of homemade conserves will line the shelves.

Cooking in the Kitchen-at-Camont is still a joy after all these years.

Kate Hill is a teacher, coach, cook, mentor, and author with more than 40 years of experience in the food world. When she isn't traveling the world giving workshops or collaborating with other leaders in her field, she runs charcuterie programs and courses at her home and school in France, the Kitchen at-Cumont. Since her arrival in 1991, Kate has forged deep ties with butchers, *charcutiers*, and other producers in Gascony and in the Basque Country. This unique combination of experience and networking has placed her at the forefront of the whole-carcass butchering movement and only further strengthens her reach as a teacher and communicator on a global scale.

Kate's work and her school, Kitchen-at-Camont, have been featured in many broadcasts, including "Rick Stein's French Odyssey" on BBC Two, and ARTE TV's "Les Routes Mythiques de l'Europe." She has also been featured in *Food & Wine*, *Bon Appétit*, *Dish*, *Appellation*, *Maison Sud Ouest*, the *New York Times*, the *Los Angeles Times*, *The Times* (UK), the *Boston Globe, and* a collaboration with Michael Ruhlman for *Condé Nast Traveler*.

Currently, she is the CEO of Grrls Meat Camp, an international organization that aims to inspire, instruct and initiate a sisterhood of farmers, butchers, cooks, and teachers giving voice to women working with food animals and meat.

For more information, please check out her website at *www.kitchen-at-camont.com*.

ACKNOWLEDGMENTS

This little book is a witness to the friendships and relationships built across a bowl of cassoulet—all this from the simple peasant dish of beans and meat that has pulled people to my table at Camont in Southwest France as I've traveled across the global kitchen. Making cassoulet a verb has been my own obsession, the very act of gathering together to celebrate good, distinctive, and regional food. The recipes in this book document the gatherings and celebrations of life at Camont and I am grateful for all those who have cooked with me, eaten with me, and done the dishes.

Thank you to the Not brothers, Aimé and Robert, and now the next-generation cousins, Jean-Pierre and Phillipe, who guided my hand each time I cradled one of their hand-thrown clay *cassoles*. The shape, heft, and volume of the empty bowls are the physical promise of a delicious cassoulet to come—my obligation to their craft.

I learned more about beans from pal Steve Sando, the king of Rancho Gordo's heirloom beans, than from all the cookbooks combined. Thanks, Steve, for your love of beans. Your passion fueled my desire to understand the "why" of the bean—the French Cassoulet bean in particular.

I am ever grateful to Tim Clinch who has photographed more bowls of brown food than any talented photographer should have to (willingly) and contributed to the *bonhomie* at each and every tasting. His photographs of the good food of Southwest France, and the people who grow it, showcase his love of the region as well as his talents.

And an extra special *merci* to Katie Hunter and Nathan Gilmour—Team Camont—who helped wrestle the text and photographs into this tidy package of savory goodness and into our eager hands. Understanding the meaning of "finish," they stand for all the good projects that come out of our Kitchen-at-Camont.

Of course, all errors are my responsibility, and any misinformation or mythology about cassoulet's murky past are my own invention and obsession.

— *Kate Hill*
November 8, 2015

INDEX

H

Ham bones and salt-cured ends
for charcuterie, 68–69
Faux Cassoulet Pork and Beans,
119–120
Ham hocks (*jarret*), 66, 68, 72
Haricots de Maïs. See Tarbais beans
Herbs and spices, 86
Hill, Kate, 137

I

Ingredients
basics, 45–46
controversy about, 20, 23–24, 27
herbs and spices, 86
seasonings, 58, 81–86
water, 82
See also Bean varieties;
Charcuterie; Duck confit
(*confit de canard*)

J

Jarret (ham hocks), 66, 68, 72

K

Kidney beans, white, 53
Kitchen-at-Camont
about, 132–133
bean varieties grown at, 53
Camp Cassoulet, 27
Kate Hill, 137
water characteristics, 82

L

Lamb, as charcuterie, 72, 75
Languedoc (France), 20
Lingot beans, 24, 50, 51

M

Montagné, Prosper, 75

N

Navy beans, 54
Not, Emile, Aimé, and Robert, 37–38
Not, Jean-Pierre and Phillipe, 38

O

Occitan language, *caçola*
(cooking dish), 33

P

Pois carré beans (cow peas), 19
Pork
bones used in broth, 66
Chapolard Family and, 66, 77–78
couenne (fresh pork rind), 71, 99
Faux Cassoulet Pork and Beans,
119–120
ham bones and salt-cured ends,
68–69
ham hocks (*jarret*), 66, 68, 72
pigs' feet, ears, tail, 69
ventrèche, 68, 99, 124, 128
See also Charcuterie
Poterie Not Frères, 37–38